SIMPLY

1 Mom's Thoughts About Coping When an Adult Child Lives With Mental Illness

STACY A. KING

Also by Stacy A. King

THE LUGGAGE DROP: A NOVEL

Note: In 2010, I found my oldest daughter near death after a suicide attempt. She was twenty years old at the time.

Somehow, by the grace of God, she miraculously survived. Even so, as a parent, I found myself struggling because of the traumatic event. A year later, after months of healing, I rented blog space on the worldwide web and named my space Stacy's Flutterings. I did this with two goals in mind:

- I wanted to let other parents know—who are walking a similar walk—that they are not alone.

- And I wanted to share credible mental health resources that have helped me and my family.

Now, four years later, I've weaved some of my most read blog posts into a guide I've titled *Simply 1 Mom's Thoughts About Coping When an Adult Child Lives With Mental Illness*. As you read through the guide, you will notice that most chapters end with what I call Stacy's Flutterings blog snapshots. They are blog posts that are old now but that are just as pertinent today as the day I wrote them. And I hope you will see the value in them as well. In closing, as you embark on reading the pages ahead, remember— you are not alone, friend. You've got this!

Disclaimer

This book, *Simply 1 Mom's Thoughts About Coping When an Adult Child Lives With Mental Illness*, is not intended as a substitute for medical and/or therapeutic advice. Readers are reading and/or using any of the information they glean from this book at their own risk. Readers should consult with a doctor and/or therapist in matters relating to parenting an adult child who lives with mental illness. The thoughts shared in this book are simply thoughts from a mother who has lived experience with the mental illness of an adult child, and those thoughts are not meant to be construed otherwise. Furthermore, the author makes no representation or warranties with respect to the accuracy, applicability, or completeness of the contents of this book. The information contained in this book is for educational and inspirational purposes only. Therefore, if you wish to apply ideas contained in this book, you are taking full responsibility for your actions.

For Bill,
Thank you to the love of my life for believing in me and
encouraging me to follow my dreams. You are my life.

For Paul, Kim and Katlin,
Thank you for allowing me to share our story. I am so
proud of each of you! I can't believe that I have the
privilege of being your mother! I love each of you
beyond measure!

For Marissa and Jaden,
You are my sunshine!

Contents

Introduction

I've heard over the years, from family and friends, the African proverb that it takes a village to raise a child. I tend to agree. We don't parent in a vacuum. By the time a child is grown many people have come and gone from a child's life. The interesting thing is, once a child is grown, it seems that the village disappears. In America, when a child turns eighteen years old, we consider the child to be an adult and as such the child is expected to act accordingly. With adulthood comes independence; no longer is the same level of parental support and help needed—or so the story goes. However, what if the child, now an adult, lives with the continuation of or the recent onset of mental illness? Now what?

Who do parents turn to for information if their child, now grown, lives with mental illness? We know children aren't born with a manual that describes how to raise them. We simply do the best we can with what we have. During our child's younger years we have doctors, teachers, family and others to reach out to. However, once our child reaches the adulthood milestone, it seems that as parents we have nowhere to turn because our child is an *adult*. As an adult they are responsible for making their own decisions, and they legally have the right to do so. What can seem like murky territory can become even murkier.

Welcome! My name is Stacy King, and I'm the author of *Simply 1 Mom's Thoughts About Coping When an Adult Child Lives With Mental Illness.* And I'm a wife and mother of three remarkable adult children: a son and two daughters. It just so happens that our middle child lives with bipolar disorder. I know what it's like to raise children, and I can empathize with parents who have an adult child who lives with mental illness.

In my experience, life can become very uncertain when a child becomes an adult, and it can become even more uncertain when a child lives with mental illness. In fact, that's why I wrote this book. My hope is twofold:

1. I hope this book will shed positive light on the murky territory of parenting an adult child who lives with mental illness.
2. I hope this book can help you navigate this uncertain time in your adult child's life.

I've been there. I'm there now. I'm surviving. And I'd like to share with you how I'm surviving. The village is still here. It just looks a little different.

Please remember, I'm simply 1 mom. I'm not a doctor or therapist. I'm offering my perspective as a mother. I highly encourage anyone going through a similar experience to visit with a doctor and/or therapist for ideas on how best to cope, especially due to the uniqueness of each individual and each individual's situation.

Wishing you and your loved ones all the very best.

Stacy- Simply 1 Mom

1

You Are Not Alone

I imagine you are reading this book because you, just like me, have an adult child who lives with mental illness or maybe it appears to you that your adult child may be living with an undiagnosed mental illness. Perhaps you are a relative or a friend who knows someone who has an adult child who lives with mental illness. Maybe you are a professional. Regardless of who you are, I'm glad you are here, and I hope that you find the book to be helpful.

For those parents who have an adult child who lives with mental illness, I just want to share with you that I'm so sorry for any challenges you've faced past and present. I know what it's like, and it's not easy. Even though it might not seem like it—you are not alone.

My daughter, Kim, also known as our songbird, lives with bipolar disorder. She was officially diagnosed with bipolar disorder when she was nineteen years old. She's twenty-six years old now. Up until the time of her diagnosis, she had been battling depression and suicidal ideations as well. Furthermore, she is also a suicide survivor. She miraculously survived her last, near fatal, attempt. That was in 2010. Whatever your story may be, just know we walk a similar walk.

How do I know we walk a similar walk? The proof is in the numbers. If we just look at how many people are affected by bipolar disorder globally, the numbers are staggering. The World Health Organization notes that about 60 million people worldwide are affected by bipolar affective disorder (World Health Organization [WHO], 2015). Can you imagine the number of people affected by mental illness if we add in all of the other mental illnesses? It's eye opening, isn't it? And each one of these millions of individuals, living with bipolar disorder, has a parent. I'm not saying the parent is involved in their lives or anything about parenting other than the fact that each person has a parent, biological or not and absent or not.

I've proven we are not alone as parents of an adult child who lives with mental illness, yet it doesn't feel that way, does it? Over the years, as we've coped with the illness of our daughter, we've felt very alone, and to some degree we are. Of course, no one else can live our lives and therefore experience what we experience. Despite this reality, I have to admit there are times I wish others could see—and actually feel—what we live through so they could understand us better.

Actually, wishing others could *live* our reality when times are tough gets to the heart of empathy. How can others empathize with me and my family if they don't know what we've experienced? The truth is, no one really can. The closest we can come to true empathy is to share our story with others living a similar story. That's precisely what I'm doing because I don't want you to feel any more alone than I did. When times get tough, and you are feeling isolated, remember you are not alone.

2

Embrace Your Normal

I don't know about you, but for me, life hasn't turned out the way that I thought it would. When I met, fell in love with, married and started a family with Bill, I didn't give much thought to where we would be as a couple and as a family unit once the kids grew up—other than what's considered the norm. When the kids were younger, Bill and I talked about short and long term goals for the both of us and the kids. And I had the usual worries, as many parents do, about the safety and well-being of our children. Of course, I imagined that once we raised the kids, the kids would go off to college and begin their lives as adults.

I selfishly admit, I used to imagine that once the kids were grown, Bill and I could be found on a comfortably cool, slightly breezy sunny afternoon sitting on rocking chairs outside on a front porch enjoying one another's company while drinking coffee and talking about life. That's it. There wasn't much more to it. Sounds good, doesn't it? That was my idea of how I thought life would turn out to be. That was in the late 1980's.

What I thought would be *our normal* would change significantly by the time Bill and I moved our family from Wyoming to Illinois. When we moved to Illinois, in 2001, we ended up moving a couple of times before settling down and buying a home in the town of O'Fallon. In fact, we lived in O'Fallon temporarily and then moved to Shiloh and then back to O'Fallon again which is where we decided to settle and thus purchase a home. Kim said that it was while we lived in Shiloh, in 2002, that she started to experience depression. She was in sixth grade. At that time, Bill and I didn't know that she was experiencing such emotional turmoil. All we knew was something had changed in regard to her behavior. Our move to Shiloh marked the beginning of some tumultuous times with Kim.

Six years later Kim would graduate from high school, but instead of graduating with a diploma and a letter jacket, as some kids do, and like our son did, she graduated with a diploma and a royal blue embroidered chenille letter "O" that has a gold colored felt edge. The letter is about 7.5 inches long by 6.5 inches wide, and the word "CHOIR" is stamped near the bottom of the "O." The letter "O" stands for the first letter in OTHS (O'Fallon Township High School), and it was meant for the jacket we never bought her because we were busy trying to survive those trying years with her while attempting to effectively continue to care for Paul and Katlin and take care of our marital relationship as well. We never even bought Katlin a letter jacket.

Important to note, I know that letter jackets are not the ultimate goal for high school graduates. In fact, Kim almost didn't graduate from high school due to her illness. Therefore, I appreciate the hard work that it takes for any student to earn his or her high school diploma. I just wanted to share the story of the letter jacket letter because I think the letter "O," that Kim was awarded for her participation in choir, is symbolic of a critical time in my family's life. I'll do my best to explain what I mean in the following paragraphs.

It was during our kid's high school years that Bill and I noticed that it seemed like other parents were experiencing the norm. It appeared that their kids grew up, graduated high school, started college, moved out and the rest was history. Raising their children seemed almost uneventful for them. We knew of parents who had children who had been accepted to the colleges of their choice and yet other parents who had children who were planning on attending college locally. We knew of other parents who had children who had decided to join the armed forces and so on and so forth.

Why was it that our story seemed so different? Our family wasn't focused on college and/or careers for the kids. Our family was focused on survival. Our growth as individuals, and as a family, seemed stunted. We seemed to be stuck—and at times we didn't know how to move forward.

After Kim's high school graduation, the difficult times didn't end. Kim ended up being diagnosed with bipolar disorder, and she attempted to take her life, not once but several times. Her last attempt, in May of 2010, was near fatal. After taking over ninety of her psychotropic medications, she ended up on life support. Even Poison Control didn't have an answer regarding how to best treat her. Her life depended on the skills of the ER staff treating her. Our beautiful songbird had temporarily ceased to sing.

As I shared with you in the first chapter, she miraculously survived. It's now 2015, and she's been stable for several years now, and we take things one day at a time. She currently resides with Bill and I, and she has hopes of becoming self-sufficient soon. Bill and I remain hopeful that she will be able to take care of herself and her own little one. She's making great strides to do so, and she has so much potential. She's worked hard to repair and strengthen her voice. She's writing original music and singing like never before. Our beautiful songbird sings again. We are very proud of her just like her siblings. She will make it! She's come so far! How can she not?

Fast forward to the present, and as you can see, our story definitely unfolded differently than I had imagined it would all those years ago when Bill and I first started our family. In regard to the letter jacket letter "O," the royal blue letter can be found partially sticking out of a small wooden basket filled with other mementos that sits on top of an antique, Birdseye Maple dresser in my bedroom. With its gold colored felt edges, now embellished with years of dust and slight wrinkles and folds, I see it as symbolic of the fact that our family survived, intact, the tumultuous years that followed after we moved to

Shiloh, I see it as symbolic of the fact that by the time Kim graduated high school she had survived depression, self-harm and suicidal ideations, and it's symbolic of the fact that she has survived several suicide attempts in the years after graduating from high school. We may not have had the same experiences as other parents, but I'm okay with that now.

I've opened up and shared a little about our story with great purpose. Yes, *our normal* has changed, but I have good news for parents who have been through a similar experience with their children. I've come to embrace *our normal*, and I encourage you to embrace *your normal* as well. When you embrace *your normal* there is so much freedom to gain. It is what it is. No longer will you compare yourself or your adult kids to others. If you are like me, you won't want to. Stand tall on the foundation you built. It may have cracks in it, but those cracks are evidence that you've survived, and you are continuing to grow. If we dismiss all of our hard work, including the very foundation we stand on, and its cracks, we won't get very far because it takes a foundation from which to begin. Be proud, and embrace *your normal*.

For additional insight, I'm closing this chapter with a Stacy's Flutterings blog snapshot that I hope will inspire you to embrace *your normal*. And by the way, that dream I used to have about Bill and I sitting outside on a sunny day enjoying a cup of coffee together while talking about life? It happens often. It just looks a little different. Instead of rocking chairs, we have stationary wicker chairs, and instead of using the front porch, we like to use the back porch. And instead of it just being Bill and I, many times Kim joins us and so does our beautiful two-year old granddaughter. And it's wonderful. Dreams do come true.

OUR NORMAL

September 5, 2011

I was talking to Bill last Wednesday night about something that came up with Kim. He asked me why I was explaining the situation to him. Actually, it is something that has continued to be a common thread and is a consequence of bipolar disorder. I explained that I thought he should be aware of what had just occurred. He gently replied, "Honey, it's our normal." He is so right! We have what we call "our normal." It sure isn't what we thought it would be, but it is definitely okay. Bill and I have accepted the fact that life has not turned out as we thought it would, and that works for us. It took us several years to get to this point. However, we did, and I am proud of the both of us for reaching this time in our lives together. Instead of running, when things get tough, we readjust and try to remain neutral knowing that some things we just can't change. However, we can adjust.

Adjust is what we have done. I am proud that we have done this together. I admit that we've had times where, instead of running from an extremely challenging situation, we actually have collided. We are both different people. Yes, Bill is male, and I am female, but it's more than that. We each have our own ideas on how we think things should be in regard to our kids as well as a multitude of other life situations and events, but somehow we have met in the middle. We have reached a consensus. That consensus is that we have what we call "our normal." I love "our normal." It means that we are still together as a couple, and therefore, we are still together as a family. Our strength, hopefully, will help our family continue to move through life regardless of what comes our way.

I have a motto I live by now. My motto is: remain neutral, readjust if necessary and remember, it's our normal. It isn't just any normal. It's "our normal."

3

Get Organized

As the parent of an adult child who lives with mental illness, I've discovered that home management can be quite challenging at times. Add into the mix that Kim still lives at home, and organization of anything in the house seems to fly out the window more often than not. Try as I might, I can't seem to keep anything in its designated place for long. It's not that Kim isn't organized. It's just the nature of several people living together. I imagine that you know what I mean if your situation is similar. There is one particular item that is a constant battle, and that my friend is paperwork. At times, we have so much paperwork that our household seems to be swimming in it.

Important to note, I'm not complaining about managing my household. In fact, I find it humorous at times. I just want to address this concern with you in an effort to share how I cope with the challenge of home management, specifically in regard to paperwork, just in case my idea can be of help to you. The reason I want to focus on paperwork is that I know what it's like to have paperwork pile up that belongs to an adult child that is of a medical nature.

Regarding paperwork in general, in addition to my paperwork and Bill's, Kim's paperwork is oftentimes a part of the mix. And now we have our granddaughter's paperwork to contend with as well. Actually, we are currently experiencing an overabundance of paperwork once again. We just recently moved into a new house, and as a consequence, we have piles of paperwork randomly showing up. If you were at my house, right at this very moment, you would see paperwork on the kitchen counter, on my home office desk, on my dresser and on Kim's dresser. Do I dare say that you might even see paperwork on my bathroom counter? It pertains to medication, but its paperwork! I should have my pilot (pile it) license by now, as my mother-in-law would say. We have mail piled here, piled there and piled everywhere! I have faith that here soon, after we finish unpacking and moving in, that I will be able to get our paperwork organized once again.

In regard to the significance of Kim's paperwork, I'm not just talking about her bills. I'm talking about the fact that at times, especially in the past, we've had to contend with her hospital discharge paperwork, physician and therapist documentation, medical insurance paperwork, medication guides, documentation pertaining to resources and anecdotal notes and more. As I've grappled with her medical paperwork, I've discovered that it doesn't fit neatly into a file folder. Yes, I could file her paperwork according to different categories, but rather than that, I came up with another idea.

The idea that I came up with, to help organize Kim's paperwork, is not some new and catchy organizational trend but rather a simple idea that I had learned and utilized as a student. As a student, I organized my papers using a binder. Do you remember doing this too? It sounds mundane, but it works great and has been an important tool in our parenting toolbox. What better place to safely keep a substantial amount of paperwork. All of her paperwork is organized in the binder categorically. It's easy for us to refer back to and easy to store. It fits neatly in a safe or in another safe place. It also has an air of confidentiality to it. There is no need for a binder cover. I chose a binder, to store Kim's paperwork in that happens to be my favorite color.

Also, what is helpful about the binder is that all of her documentation is handy if we find we need it. It is one less thing that we have to be concerned about. Life is a little less cluttered, and we have time to focus on what is really important.

Lastly, having Kim's documentation organized and stored in one place gives me a sense of control at a time when I don't necessarily feel that I have control. If you too find that you are battling with your adult child's paperwork, and you feel out of control, maybe you could organize his or her paperwork in a similar fashion.

Those who haven't walked in our shoes quite possibly wouldn't understand how something so simple could help us feel like we have some semblance of control. That's okay. What matters is now. So let's take control, and get that paperwork organized! You and your family are worth it. And stay tuned! In the next chapter, I talk more about regaining a sense of control.

4

Knowledge Really Is Power

How many times have you heard Francis Bacon's famous quote, "Knowledge is power?" I imagine that you've heard this quote a zillion times like I have. I know I'm being overzealous by saying "zillion," but I think you know what I mean. Despite that it's a quote many of us have heard over and over, I have to admit that I believe knowledge really is power, especially for those of us who happen to have an adult child who lives with mental illness.

Whether or not your adult child lives with an official diagnosis, was just recently diagnosed or remains undiagnosed, I encourage you to learn all you can about your child's illness. Why? There are several benefits to doing so such as: regaining a sense of control, developing the ability to recognize symptoms so that you can intervene if necessary, developing the ability to begin to understand what works and what doesn't work regarding communication and developing the ability to provide meaningful support. And of utmost importance, by learning all you can about your child's illness, you will see that your child is human. How can I prove to you that knowledge really is power? Keep reading.

First, in regard to regaining a sense of control, it was when I began the journey to learn all I could about my daughter's mental illness, after her last suicide attempt, that I began to regain a sense of control at a time when I felt I had none. It was on the morning of May 21st, 2010 at 7:20 AM that I felt I had lost all control as a parent. That was the morning that I found Kim after she had attempted suicide the evening before by taking over ninety of her psychotropic medications. She was near deaths door by the time I found her. What power did I have as a parent the moment that I found her? All I had was enough strength to yell for Bill's help. And I had just enough strength to call 911. However, I didn't have the power to stop what she had done, and I certainly didn't have the power to stop what was in motion. As a parent—I had become powerless.

What saddened me and pained me more, at that time, was that life effortlessly marched on literally and figuratively speaking all around me while Kim laid in an emergency room in a drug induced coma on life support. While everyone around me, including our family and her friends, went about their lives, not knowing what she had done, there Bill, Paul, Katlin and I were standing over her hospital bedside watching a cold alien like sterile machine breathe for her and keep her alive.

At that time, I experienced a swirl of feelings that I'd never felt before as a mother. I felt oddly disconnected from her yet intimately connected to her as well. Who was this girl who looked like Sleeping Beauty, and would she awake? I had so many questions and no answers. That's what led me to learn as much as I could about mental illness in general, bipolar disorder, anxiety disorder and suicide prevention. That was almost five years ago.

Fast forward to today, and to be honest, I still experience moments of feeling out of control. Let me see if I can explain. As the parent of an adult child who lives with mental illness, there are times that I find myself feeling as if I don't have control of my life. I am forty-eight years old. I'm married. I have three grown children and two granddaughters. I own my home with my husband and so on and so forth. How can it be that at forty-eight years old—I don't feel that I'm in control of my life?

Well, one of my adult children still lives at home with me, and therefore, one of my granddaughter's lives with me. The house is in a constant state of clutter, my husband and I have little privacy, and basically, Bill and I can't do anything the way that we want to. It sounds selfish, but it's a fact. At the age of forty-eight, I can't do what I want for the most part, when I want. Then you add in that I can't make my daughter well when she's feeling ill. As a mother, this is an awful feeling. When she was a little one, I was able to kiss her boo boos away. And now, it seems that if anything, I have the tendency to make the situation worse sometimes when she's not feeling well.

Ah, control. It sounds so good, doesn't it? This is the point where I have good news pertaining to control. Believe it or not, as parents, we do have control. It just looks a little different. For example, we have control over our decisions, good and bad. We also have control over our actions. We also have control over certain areas of our lives. It's just a matter of learning what it is that we can control.

And now, it's in your hands to learn what it is in your life that you control. A great book to start with is titled *Stop Walking on Eggshell*s by Paul T. Mason and Randi Kreger. The mental illness, that is the focus of the book, is borderline personality disorder, but I think that you will find valuable information pertaining to your situation as well. I know I did, and I highly recommend it to you. At the very least, Paul T. Mason and Randi Kreger give you permission to take back your life, if that's of concern.

Second, in regard to developing the ability to recognize symptoms, if you want to help your adult child, it's prudent to learn all you can about the mental illness your adult child lives with. The reason that I think we, as parents, should learn all we can about our adult child's mental illness is so that we can intervene if necessary. For example, had I known that Kim was exhibiting some of the signs of an impending suicide attempt, I would have at least known that I needed to have her evaluated by her psychiatrist and/or therapist at minimum.

What's perplexing, to me as a mother, is that I knew that she was acting differently such as the fact that she was acting more depressed, more withdrawn, and she had increased her use of drugs. However, I didn't react. Instead, I chose to remain confused and did nothing other than express my concerns to Bill. What was I thinking? If only I had known the warning signs of suicide maybe I could have stopped her from doing what she did. I didn't know the signs, and I almost lost her. This is frightening, isn't it?

You don't have to have a similar experience. Learn all you can about the signs and symptoms of whatever your child is battling. Your knowledge could save your child's life.

Third, in regard to developing the ability to begin to understand what works and what doesn't work regarding communication, I highly encourage you to learn how to communicate with your adult child. Had my communication skills been better, maybe I would have been able to encourage Kim to seek help. For example, if I would have been familiar with the Depression and Bipolar Support Alliance (DBSA) guide titled "What Helps and What Hurts" maybe I would have said something different to Kim the night that she made the near fatal suicide attempt. For instance, that evening, I had noticed that she was behaving differently so I decided to check on her before I went to bed. When I checked in on her, I found her in her bed crying. I asked her what was wrong. After a few moments she said, through her tears, "I love you, Mom." I said, "I love you too, sweetie." I then asked her if there was anything that I could do. That was it, nothing more. She replied tearfully, "No." I replied, "Okay. I'll be upstairs if you need me." I kissed her on her forehead and walked away.

My friend, I walked away while she was crying. Again, what was I thinking? I ignored every sign that there was something wrong. I even ignored my gut instinct that was telling me that something was seriously wrong. Was I in denial? I don't know. I think so. Was I ignorant? Yes. Kim's life, like a discarded smoldering campfire flame was extinguishing right in front of me, and I did nothing. Instead of walking away, I could have said, "Let's talk. I'm listening." I understand that this is conjecture, and I'll never know whether or not had I communicated differently with her would have changed the outcome, but what if I would have known how to communicate better? What if?

Fourth, in regard to developing the ability to provide meaningful support, had I known what I know now, I think that I would have been able to provide Kim with support that mattered and would have helped. When she was in the throes of her illness, I impeded her wellness rather than helped. Instead of taking the time to listen to her, I oftentimes talked over her. I expected her to listen to me. It made sense to me at the time. I'm the parent, right? That being said, I have the last say, right? Wrong. I only wish I would have read, the DBSA guide, "Helping Others Throughout Their Lives: What Can I Do When My Child Is Ill?" Had I read this guide, I would have understood it's best to treat our adult children like adults. That's how I expect to be treated. Why did I think it was different with my adult children? What a difference this simple change could have made. If only I knew then what I know now maybe she would have come to me regarding the suicidal ideations she was experiencing.

Fifth, in regard to the humanizing of our adult children, over the years as I've learned as much as I can about mental illness, bipolar disorder, anxiety and suicide prevention, I've noticed something extremely important about my daughter and that is—she's human. She is not her illness. She is Kim, and she is beautiful, and she is strong. She just happens to live with bipolar disorder and anxiety, and it's okay. It's not the end of the world. She just needs treatment at times just like if she had diabetes. Mental illness is just that. It's an illness, nothing more. That girl who I saw in the hospital on the 21st of May in 2010 who looked like Sleeping Beauty—she's human and she's awake.

Before moving on, I think it's important that I share with you that I don't blame myself for Kim's mental illness or her suicide attempts. Would I change how I parented her before learning what I know now? You bet I would. However, I can't change the past. What I can change is today. I choose to continue to expand my knowledge about mental illness and suicide prevention and apply what I'm learning as I go.

I hope you can glean something from this chapter that will help you as well. And as a reminder, I'm simply 1 mom sharing her thoughts. As such, I'm not a professional. I'm just a parent sharing my experiences. Therefore, I encourage you to discuss these ideas with a professional. Your doctor and/or therapist will be able to help you navigate any trying times and come up with a plan of action. As we move forward, as parents of adult children who live with mental illness—let's not forget that we are human too.

5

Take Care of You

Sydney Harris said it perfectly when he said, "The time to relax is when you don't have time for it." If you are like me, and I imagine many of you are, you are busy taking care of everyone else but you. Does this sound about right? I can't express enough how important it is that you take care of yourself, especially if you are coping with an adult child who lives with mental illness.

I have discovered, over the years, that it's too easy to get swept up taking care of my loved one to the point that I have forgotten to take care of myself. What usually happens is that I end up having a meltdown of sorts because I can't possible continue to carry the emotional weight of my daughter and everyone else as well. When I have a meltdown, it's unhealthy for me, my daughter and everyone else. The good news is that it doesn't have to be this way. Let's remember to take care of ourselves so that in turn we are the best we can be for adult children who at times may need our strength, energy, love and support.

Below is a Stacy's Flutterings blog snapshot that highlights the importance of taking care of you.

YOU HAVE PERMISSION TO RELAX AND DE-STRESS NOW: CREATING MOMENTS OF RESPITE

September 5, 2011

Do you make time for yourself to de-stress? What's great is that if you don't, you have permission to relax and de-stress now. Yes, you can relax and de-stress at this very moment. How? Keep reading.

Taking a moment to relax and de-stress is also known as respite. With this in mind, and in recognition of National Stress Awareness Day, I thought I'd share this post with you about respite care. So what is respite care, and how does it apply to our lives? According to ARCH National Respite Network and Resource Center, respite is "planned or emergency care provided to a child or adult with special needs in order to provide temporary relief to family caregivers who are caring for that child or adult" (n.d.). Merriam-Webster.com defines respite as "an interval of rest or relief" (n.d).

Hmmm...rest...relief...sounds wonderful, doesn't it? Below you will find my story of how I discovered that we can actually create moments of personal respite on a daily basis. Yes, planned respite is needed and an integral part of care-giving. However, we can also intentionally create personal moments of respite throughout each and every day to help us survive daily stressors. How? Well...

I recently saw one of my doctor's for a follow up appointment. I asked him if the symptoms I have been experiencing could be brought on by stress. Before he could answer my question, I anxiously blurted out that I have been experiencing a great deal of stress. As I busily talked with my hands, as I so often do, he politely took the time to listen to my story, and he calmly said, "Stacy, while you are here at our office, use the time to relax and breathe."

I was kind of taken aback. I didn't expect him to say that. He gave me permission to relax. I felt a sense of calm wash over me. As his words sunk into my stress laden brain, I took a deep breath and exhaled. It was as if someone had taken a fresh warm blanket out of the dryer on an icy cold December day and wrapped it around me. Any tension I felt left my body, and I felt a little less stressed.

As a wife, mother, grandmother, caregiver, friend, etc., I oftentimes forget to take care of myself. Usually, it takes me getting sick or hurt to realize that I need to slow down and refocus a little on myself. It is interesting to me that sometimes we need someone to give us permission to do something so simple as relax.

Since that day at the doctor's office, I have come to realize that we have the power to create personal moments of respite. If we are at the doctor's office, we can use that time, as my doctor said, to relax. We can turn a sometimes unpleasant situation, like a waiting room, into a moment of respite. We can capture the moments that oftentimes elude us and recreate a moment to just inhale and exhale the stress.

So here's to creating personal moments of respite in an effort to be the best we can be for the amazing people in our lives, including ourselves!

6

Seek Help from Others

Did you cringe when you saw the title of this chapter? I'll be honest with you. I cringed at the thought of saying, "Seek help from others." It's not easy, and I know it's not. The last thing that I wanted to be told when I was in the midst of turmoil in regard to my daughter's mental illness was to seek help from others. That was actually the last thing I wanted to hear and do, and if I had my way, I wasn't going to seek help. At that time, I wasn't able to help myself much less my daughter so who in their right mind would think that someone else could help us. That was then. This is now.

Below is a Stacy's Flutterings blog snapshot that touches on this important topic. I hope that it inspires you to reach out to others, especially during trying times. Support from others can be priceless.

THE PRAYER SHAWL: A GLIMPSE INTO THE WORLD OF SUPPORT FROM OTHERS

May 14, 2014

In recognition of APA's Your Mind Your Body Mental Health Blog Day May 14th, 2014, I've decided to write about support. Writing about support has lingered in my mind ever since I rediscovered the prayer shawl that my son had given me after my daughter's last hospitalization a few years ago.

When everything in our world seemed to crumble, in regard to our daughter's mental health, it was my son who introduced me to the idea of support from others. I didn't realize it at the time. I was so consumed by my own grief, sadness, sense of loss and the care of my loved one that I didn't really think about much else. Our family was in survival mode. The last item on my list was support from others. To be perfectly honest, I don't think it crossed my mind. How could I reach out for support from anyone when I was so busy trying to wrap my brain around the fact that my daughter needed help beyond what I was capable of providing as a mother?

Four years have somehow slipped by since that tumultuous time in our lives. We've moved on as individuals and as a family. The good times and sad times are but mere memories, or snapshots if you will, of life lived. Memories are tucked away in our preconscious minds, material objects from days gone by are stored as objects to be seen and on display, and some objects have been carefully put away. For instance, a lighted, crystal salt lamp sits on a shelf as a reminder of the first family trip we took to Branson, Missouri after Kim's last attempt. It was purchased in Branson during that trip with purpose. It sits with a warm, glowy presence on a shelf in our family living room as a testament to our family's commitment to one another. Its rugged landscape represents the difficult times we experience as a family unit. And it's singularity as one piece of crystal salt represents how we always seem to come together when one of us is in need. And then there are those items that are neatly and carefully stowed away like the prayer shawl.

I imagine, at this point, that you may be wondering what a prayer shawl is. Within the next few paragraphs, I'll try to explain.

It was when I least expected it that I found my prayer shawl laying right where I had placed it years ago. I was busy looking for a particular item, and I thought it might be in my hope chest. I briskly walked to my room. I was on a mission to find whatever it was at the time. Once I got to the hope chest, I leaned down and pressed the button to unlock the cedar chest. As I pressed the button in, and held it, I lifted the heavy bench seat top. As the chest opened, I saw the shawl. Its vibrant magenta color caught my attention. There it was...laying there...a carefully crocheted 2 ft. by 5 ft. piece of love. As I pulled the shawl out of the cedar chest, I noticed the carefully hand stitched label on one side of the shawl that identifies the church where it came from. The shawl itself is bordered by an elegant, scalloped crocheted edge, and it is beautiful. The lacy stitches and vivid color exude the thoughtful, loving and caring nature of the person who stitched it. And somehow, I was the blessed recipient of it, but how?

It was during the time when Kim had attempted suicide. Each of us, in our nuclear family, reacted very differently during her hospitalization as well as after. The night before Kim was brought out of the coma, Paul had left. He literally left. He couldn't take seeing his sister in a coma so through his tears, outside of Kim's ICU room separated from her by a mere curtain and beyond earshot, he said his goodbyes to Bill, Katlin and I, and he headed out of the hospital. He called me later in the evening crying as he drove. He said, "Mom, I'm so sorry. I can't take seeing Kim like that. I had to leave. I hope you and Dad understand." I told him, "I know. I love you so much, Paul! You have to take care of yourself. Just let Dad and I know how it's going. Please keep us posted." He replied, "I will, Mom." I said, "I love you, Paul." His last reply was, "I love you too, Mom. Bye."

Later, I would learn that he had drove to a neighboring city to see a good friend. He didn't come back that night. Instead, somewhere in a town close by, my son sat in a church room surrounded by church goers and his friend praying that Kim would survive. The healing support that Paul had found in a neighboring town made its way to our family and embraced us warmly. When we reconnected with Paul, after that tearful night that he had decided to leave, he walked up to me and gently wrapped the beautiful, hand crocheted, magenta colored prayer shawl around my shoulders. He then told me that when I was feeling sad and down that I could use it for comfort. He told me that people at the church he attended make prayer shawls and that they had given one to Paul to give to me. He said that the person who had given him the shawl had prayed over the shawl and asked for peace and healing for our particular situation. What a beautiful gesture it was. And what a loving son I have. I felt joy and thankfulness well up within my tired and injured soul. I felt a bit revived for the days ahead.

Paul's method of coping brought wellness not only to him but to us as well. Without knowing it, Paul had delivered me more than a gift in the form of a prayer shawl. He also gave me my first glimpse into the world of support from others beyond our family and friends. I didn't understand nor appreciate at the time how important that would be later on in Kim's recovery. My son, reeling from the harm his sister did to herself, left the scene at the hospital in an effort to cope and for self-preservation, and he came back to us stronger and ready to help Kim.

I realize now, as I contemplate this beautiful gift that Paul gave me, how important support from others really is, especially during times like we have had with Kim. Regardless of anyone's situation, and regardless of what type of illness, whether physical or mental, support from others can help uplift us and help us carry on despite our greatest challenges. I know. My son taught me.

7

Have You Heard the Word Enable Yet?

In my experience, as the parent of an adult child who lives with mental illness, I have found that it's not uncommon for the word *enable* to come up in conversation with family, friends, therapists, support groups members, the general public and others. Have you had this experience as well? I was actually told once, by someone I didn't even know, that I was enabling my daughter and that eventually I would decide not to allow her in my home until she changed her behavior. How ridiculous is that? First, my husband and I will determine whether or not we are enabling, and to be perfectly honest, it's just not that easy. Maybe other parents like to show their adult children the door when the going gets tough. That's not me, and that's not my husband, and that's not how our family chooses to operate.

As you can tell, conversations about that provocative word *enable* can be difficult at best to have. Even so, as a Family Helpline volunteer, it's not unusual for me when I'm working with a parent to bring up the word *enable* because I do believe that it's an important conversation to have when parenting an adult child who lives with mental illness. It's the norm for me to share with parents that I believe that asking ourselves as parents whether or not we are enabling our children's behavior is a question unique to each family's situation. What is considered enabling behavior for one family may mean survival behavior for another family.

For example, when my daughter was experiencing suicidal ideations, and had actually acted on those ideations, I behaved differently with her as a means of her survival, especially due to the fragility of the situation. Of course, life is not static. Since it's ever-changing, I notice that it's helpful at times to stop and take note of how I'm behaving and ask myself if I'm encouraging her behavior one way or another. I think it's a difficult question to ask ourselves as parents and one that can't always be answered clearly. Important to note, I encourage you to discuss this concept with a therapist, especially due to the uniqueness of each family, each family member and each situation.

Below is a Stacy's Flutterings blog snapshot that sheds additional light on what can be a difficult topic to discuss, and you will see how my husband and I addressed our enabling behavior.

ARE WE ENABLING? WALKING THE TIGHTROPE

November 18, 2013

Have you heard the word enable yet in regard to parenting? If you find yourself wondering what enable means, according to Khaleghi, enabling means "… lending a hand to help people accomplish things they could not do by themselves. More recently, however, it has developed the specialized meaning of offering help that perpetuates rather than solves a problem" (2012). Honestly, I hadn't really thought about whether or not I enable as a parent until it was brought up at a support group meeting for families affected by mental illness.

There I sat at the meeting an exhausted and heartbroken parent with my shoulders slumped forward as if gravity had wrapped around my shoulders like a shawl and attempted to pull me down with the guilt of unsuccessful parenting. Whatever my husband and I were doing, at the time as parents, didn't seem to be helpful to our daughter in regard to her behavior. At the peak of her illness, her behaviors seemed out of control. For instance, she self-medicated. Even though we tried to stop her, from abusing substances, it didn't seem to matter. Try as we might, and try we did, it seemed that we were ineffective as a parents. It was confusing because we have two other children that we seemed to raise just fine. However, with my middle child, we were faced with challenges that we did not expect. When she was diagnosed with bipolar disorder, we had to figure out what that meant. We had so much to learn. It seemed that we were in survival mode. We didn't even think about our parenting skills. It didn't come to mind in the beginning. Why would it? We were busy trying to figure out what type of help would benefit her, what type of medications she needed as well as how to cope with her symptoms and the ramifications of her illness. Our parental skills were the last thing on our mind and yet how we parent has become such an important tool as we journey forward with her.

In regard to the meeting, when the word "enable" was said it got my full attention. I sat up in my chair, leaned in towards the group and intently listed. As a result, I learned that enabling our loved ones can actually do more harm than good. Temporarily, the weight of parenting a loved one with bipolar disorder lifted. It's as if I tossed the heavy, gravity laden shawl of guilt I was carrying on my shoulders aside. When I heard the word "enable" I thought, "Maybe this is what we've been missing all along." I felt excited for the first time in a long time because I realized that there was still hope in regard to our parenting abilities. Perhaps we were enabling our daughter's behaviors. I found myself thinking, "That's it! That's the answer! We'll stop enabling her behaviors, and things will get better!" However, since that "aha!" moment, things haven't really gotten any easier. In fact, I think it actually got a little tougher because now we have to think about how we are going to approach certain situations in regard to our loved one's behavior and whether or not the boundaries my husband and I set either enable or support her.

As a consequence, knowing whether or not we enable our daughter feels like walking a tightrope. As we attempt to balance our parental boundaries, we find that we are still left wondering whether or not we are enabling. If we lean just a little one way we could lose our balance and potentially create a situation for our loved one that may be harmful. On the other hand, if we lean too far the other direction, we could be helping her greatly. There seems to be little room, if any, for inconsistency.

To tell you the truth, knowing whether or not we're enabling her behavior seems difficult to say the least. One way that my husband and I stopped enabling certain behaviors includes the fact that we stopped the flow of money. Without realizing it, we were actually supporting our daughter's self-medicating behavior. Each time we handed her money, we allowed her to self-medicate. Thus, we were in essence saying, "Don't drink, but here's the money you asked for, so go for it!" How confusing is that? I know that it doesn't take a rocket scientist to figure this out, but we were so overwhelmed by her illness, and just trying to survive as well as keep her alive, that the concept of enabling escaped us.

Since that meeting, we have approached parenting our daughter a little differently. We now ask ourselves, "What is in the best interest of our daughter?" And, "What might be the consequence if we support her actions or draw the line?" Usually, what helps us make a decision is that we also ask, "Will our actions hurt or help her?" For us, asking ourselves the question, "Are we enabling?" hasn't made parenting any easier. We are making progress though! I guess that's all that we can do as parents. And so, we continue to put one foot in front of the other as we walk the line together.

If you would like more information about enabling, I encourage you to visit with a counselor or family therapist about this very important topic.

8

Cope with Stress
by Remaining Neutral

I don't know about you, but for me, sometimes life can get a little stressful at my house. And life can get a little stressful for me out in the real world as well. Okay. Okay. I'll just admit it. Life can be stressful. If I noted all of the life stressors that I experience, the book wouldn't end. It would keep going and going. I'll save you from having to read through my stressors because I imagine that you understand exactly what I'm saying. Just for fun though, as I'm typing these very words and trying to work through writer's block, my daughter just accidently set the house alarm off!!

I had to take a break from writing, but I'm back now. What happened is that when Kim set off the house alarm, there was a domino effect. My husband, working from another location, called 911 because of an alert he received on his phone from ADT. He had texted me, when he got the alert, but I was writing the paragraph above and missed his text message so he made the decision to call 911. He called 911 back and cancelled the emergency. There you have it! Stress! There's simply no way around it. Life, in all its beauty and splendor, can be stressful. The good news is that there are healthy methods that we can use to cope with life's stressors. Stress doesn't have to negatively affect us anymore.

In regard to coping with stress, I'm excited to share with you a method that I learned while in the throes of Kim's illness. What it boils down to is that the coping mechanism I'm about to share with you is simply a way of reacting to stress while in the midst of stress, and what's great is that, it's free. It won't cost you anything other than being mentally present while in the stressful moment. Are you ready? Drum roll please. When I'm experiencing stress, I try and remain neutral. That's it. There's nothing more to it. Instead of being reactive, which is easy to do, I try to mentally take note of what is happening and then calm my nerves by not reacting. I do my best to remain neutral. I admit that this isn't easy to do, but it works for me.

To be honest, there are times that I don't apply this method, but when I do, it sure helps me get through a stressful situation with ease. Also, I've discovered that the more I practice choosing to remain neutral, rather than being reactive while in a stressful situation, the less I find that I have to think about it. It has become almost second nature for me. I encourage you to give it a try. Also, I encourage you to visit with a doctor and/or therapist about this coping method. Your doctor and/or therapist may have others ideas regarding how to cope with stress that you'd like to try.

Important to note, I want to share with you that I'm not trying to say that we shouldn't feel. That's part of being human. What I'm trying to say is that when we are feeling stressed, one way to handle the stress is to *choose* to react differently. When I choose to remain neutral, when faced with a stressor, I find that I react in a healthier manner: I become a better listener, I respond in a calm manner, I'm able to problem solve, and overall I feel better because the outcome is usually better.

The Stacy's Flutterings blog snapshot below provides further insight into what I'm trying to share, and encapsulates how I cope with stress.

COPING WITH STRESS
BY GLIDING ON NEUTRALITY

February 24, 2012

It seems that with the insurmountable life stressors that are bombarding me lately, I would grow frazzled and lose my mental footing on life. Surprisingly, it is quite the opposite. Instead of blindly teetering on the edge of loose and crumbly negativity, I maintain my composure by choosing mental flexibility and allowing myself to move along the treacherous whitecaps of stress as if I were gliding on a smooth, glassy reflection of a river… a river I like to call neutrality.

I could go on and on…explaining the different stressors in my life from the minuteness of running late to a doctor's appointment yesterday to the immense stress from coping with the mental illness of a loved one. But I won't. I want to focus on that very moment when life seems to kick us another curve ball called stress. What do we do? How do we handle it? Where do we go? I used to react physically, mentally and emotionally. At times I would run from stress by literally walking away. At other times I would cope with stress through denial. And at other times, I would breakdown emotionally. Depending on the stressor, at the time, I reacted with equal intensity like an opera singer…sometimes timidly like the musical notation pp Pianissimo …sometimes my stress level and reaction would crescendo like the musical notation ff Fortissimo. Not today.

Today, I react very differently. The stress of yesterday, today and tomorrow gracefully lifts and is carried away as I cope with whatever comes my way. How did I get here? It wasn't easy – that's for sure. I just decided that in the midst of the stress storm, I would not take part in equal reaction. I used to almost feed the storm with my negative reactions. Now, when I am presented with any kind of stress, I remain calm and neutral. I'm not relenting, believe me! You see, the stress storm can no longer build in intensity and rain its darkness on me leaving me powerless. I do at times vent. I do at times cry. But now I am stronger knowing that I have control over the stressors of my life. I can't stop them, but I sure can mentally glide along the smooth, glassy reflection of neutrality and face them…the insurmountable becomes possible.

9

Whose Crisis Is It Anyway?

Years ago, without knowing it, my husband Bill taught me an important concept. The concept he taught me is that when we are experiencing something that we consider to be a *crisis*, it's our crisis. Our crisis doesn't belong to anyone else. It's not their crisis. They have their own crises to deal with. This concept has been very important for me to learn because as the parent of an adult child who lives with mental illness, there are times when I wish others could help us. However, in reality, they can't because whatever the situation is, it's for us individually and as a family to cope with and not someone else.

I don't think that Bill knows it, but this extremely important concept that he taught me, and that I apply when needed, gives me a sense of control at times when I don't feel I have any. How powerful is that? Also, when we work through what we consider to be *our crisis*, we develop resiliency which provides us the opportunity to face the next challenge or crisis.

The Stacy's Flutterings blog snapshot below provides an example of how I applied this concept. If you feel a sense of loss of control in your life, especially in regard to your adult child who lives with mental illness, you will find that you too can regain a sense of control once again which in turn can help you face the next crisis.

ALL HANDS ON DECK! WAIT! WHOSE CRISIS IS IT ANYWAY?

February 9, 2012

A report by the Association for Psychological Science (2011) states, "Psychological scientists have found that, while going through many experiences like assault, hurricanes, and bereavement can be psychologically damaging, small amounts of trauma may help people develop resilience."

Trauma? Hmmm? Over the years we have had a lot come our way just like everybody else. The challenges of our life have been like waves along the seashore, some mighty like the shooting spree in Kansas and like the bipolar disorder of our loved one and ...some weak...like the arthritis I am now dealing with. Others, like waiting in long lines at the super market, are like granules of sand that the tide washes away.

With each challenge, and sometimes full on crisis, I recall responding as if it were everyone's crisis. In the moment, like when Bill was shot years ago, we were in crisis. Yes, we had a major life changing event happen. However, it was "our" problem. You see, for some reason it bothered me that anyone and everyone around me, especially in public, didn't get my pain. Years later, after the shooting, and well into another one of "our" problems, Bill told me, "Honey, it's our crisis. It doesn't belong to anyone else." Wow! I had never thought about that! Ever since, when something comes up that is some sort of turning point, I react much differently. Instead of expecting all hands on deck, I own it and respond accordingly. The outcome is usually much more positive.

Monday, I had an experience that reminded me of our saying, "It's our crisis." My beautiful daughter has been struggling the past few weeks with the challenges bipolar disorder can bring ashore. I called the psychiatrist's office to inquire about what steps to take since the waters have been getting kind of turbulent.

I was extremely nervous. I explained to the receptionist what was going on and my fear of what might come. The receptionist listened to me and…according to the silence…rather calmly looked at the psychiatrists schedule…or so I thought. It grew silent on the other end of the phone…I finally said, "Hello?" I then heard from the other end of the phone, "Yes…" I thought, "Okay…" then I heard, "The doctor and the therapist are both booked." The silenced continued as she reviewed her appointment book. I felt extremely anxious. In my mind, I had an emergency, and then I remembered Bill saying, "Stacy…It's our crisis." With that thought I was able to calm myself enough to get through the phone call. Within the next few minutes, the receptionist had set appointments up for my daughter with both the psychiatrist and the therapist. She made it work! I thanked her and shared with her how much I appreciated her patience with me. Had I unraveled, like a seashore squall, the outcome may have been very different. She didn't have an issue at that moment. I was the one with the issue.

Sometimes when a crisis happens, and life appears to be dancing happily like warm seashore raindrops all around me... I have to stop and remind myself, "It's my crisis..." And for the moment...I have some sense of control amongst the fear, and I continue to become more resilient...

10

Attention Please

Up until now, I've talked about myself, my family in general, and my daughter who lives with mental illness. I don't know if you've noticed it yet, but I haven't talked much about my oldest son and my youngest daughter. It's not that they aren't on my mind at any given moment. It's that my daughter, who lives with bipolar disorder and anxiety, tends to receive more attention than my other kids.

I'm not ashamed to admit this because it's unfortunately a fact and something that I have contended with throughout the years. I will say that it is a sad fact to me. I imagine, if you have more than one child, you know what I mean. Even though I'm not ashamed to admit this sad fact, I have to say, as a parent, it's a terrible feeling because I want to give each one of my children the same amount of attention, but it just hasn't worked out that way.

I understand that, in reality, we can't possibly give our children the exact same amount of attention. I barely have time for myself at times. Even so, I imagine that it's a difficult reality for many parents who have more than one child and at least one child who lives with mental illness. I don't know about for you, but while my children were growing up, the concern that I didn't, and don't, give each of my children the same amount of attention has been a common thread. Oh, how I wish the words I'm typing at this moment were different, but they aren't. This chapter is actually one of the hardest chapters for me to write. Could I have done things differently? You bet I could have. Would I have? I like to think so. However, I don't know. Therefore, I must keep moving forward and do the best that I can as a parent.

In regard to doing the best that I can as a parent, something that helps me move forward, when I'm feeling down about how much attention I give to Paul and Katlin is that I try and reframe my thoughts. Instead of thinking that I'm not giving enough attention to my children, or whatever my concern might be regarding the kids, I remind myself that Paul and Katlin are living their lives successfully, and they both appear to be very happy and content young adults. They both know how much I love and support them, and they both know that I've always been concerned about whether or not I've giving them the same amount of attention as I am giving to their sister. And, it's okay.

Furthermore, I understand that, as a parent, there are not predetermined conditions that I "must" live up to other than what is considered healthy parenting like taking the best possible care of each of my children. Of course, for me, that meant that while the kids were growing up, Bill and I had to provide food, clothing, shelter, safety, love, support, and the encouragement of socialization and learning. However, anything beyond that is a condition that I've placed upon myself. For example, the thinking that I "must" provide each of the kids my undivided attention, and the attention has to be the same for each child sounds ridiculous, doesn't it? But that's what I have done to myself for whatever reason.

For the past several years, I've been learning how to undo that type of thinking. I'm making progress. What I think now, rather than "I must..." is that it's the unconditional love that matters to my children and not how much attention I provide each of them. Of course, these are just my thoughts, but I encourage you to think about your "musts." Can you reframe them? I encourage you to talk with a therapist about this concept. It really can be life changing. There is actually a name for what I'm talking about. It's actually a type of psychotherapy called Cognitive Behavioral Therapy (CBT). The National Alliance on Mental Illness provides a brief overview that pertains to CBT. I encourage you to check it out. You just might like what you discover.

It's important for me to share with you that I don't want to invalidate the reality that Kim, at times, does need attention. That's the way it is, and to make sure she remains as healthy as she can mentally and physically, then she has my undivided attention, when and if it's necessary. I also don't want to invalidate Paul and Katlin's ability to cope with our situation either. Just as I've had to learn how to cope with Kim's mental illness, they've had to learn how to cope as well.

Regarding coping with the mental illness of our loved one, my family has come so far. The Stacy's Flutterings blog snapshot below is proof. The focus, of the blog snapshot has to do with Katlin and Kim's connection with one another as siblings, but I think it's also representative of what I'm trying to convey. Of course, a lot of time has passed since I published this blog post, but I'd like to share it with you anyway in the hope that it's helpful.

P.S. I LOVE YOU

August 21, 2011

Yesterday, while enjoying lunch with my youngest daughter Katlin, I was very moved by our conversation. As a mother, I have often found myself wondering if my adult children will remain in contact, and continue to have a close relationship with their siblings. Katlin blessed me with insight to that very thought; it was in regard to Kim's love of singing.

Like the changing of the tide, due to the challenges of bipolar disorder, Kim doesn't sing as often as she desires. Without any of us knowing, Katlin has been resourceful in finding Kim singing opportunities. I shared with Katlin how wonderful it was of her to help her sister. Katlin replied, "Well, it is something Kim wants to do. All I can do it set it up. It is up to her what she does with it." I heard love, maturity and strength in her words that I haven't heard before. She remains supportive of her sister while moving forward with her own life despite the multitude of bipolar roadblocks that have been thrown in her path. Katlin is coping beautifully, and she is a role model for me.

Katlin leads a very full life. She has moved into her first apartment and is busy working as a manager full-time in the food industry. She works a second job at the church nursery and also volunteers for the Karla Smith Foundation. However, she is unequivocally available for her sister. Their bond reminds me of a letter. A beautiful sister bond has been carefully scripted through love, friendship and encouragement. The editing includes the constant working through of the inevitable sibling quarrels, and usual family ups and downs including the bipolar moments...and yet at the end of the letter, and underscored, it appears that they never fail to mention to one another, "P.S. I love you."

11

What Are You Passionate About? Do It!

In the previous chapters, I've talked about how I cope with the mental illness of my adult child, and at times, I know that the subject matter has been emotionally charged. After all, I am talking about the mental illness of my child. Just typing the words, "the mental illness of my child" isn't easy for me, but I've managed to write about our family's experiences in regard to the mental illness of our loved one, and as you see, I'm moving forward.

As I move forward, I'm attempting to cast positive light where there seems to be none with great purpose, and that's what this chapter is all about. I want to focus on the growth that can occur, and that oftentimes does, after, or during, a difficult time in life. Instead of withering inside, like I felt I was doing at one point while coping with Kim's mental illness, give yourself permission to grow from your experience. I understand that what you are facing right now might seem insurmountable. I'm here to share with you that you can overcome whatever it is you are coping with in regard to your adult child and his or her illness, and during this difficult time, you can experience positive growth. Viktor E. Frankl said it perfectly when he said, "When we are no longer able to change a situation—we are challenged to change ourselves" (p. 112).

With Frankl's quote in mind, I'd like to share with you how I've changed myself since I'm not able to change the fact that my beautiful daughter lives with mental illness. Believe it or not, while in the midst of chaos brought on by Kim's illness, I actually discovered my purpose. And I acted on that knowledge.

At this point, I imagine that you are wondering how I discovered my purpose and what it might be. It's interesting because I was dabbling in it all along, and it simply has to do with writing. Throughout the years, I didn't take writing that seriously. While growing up, I enjoyed writing. And by the time that I had become an adult, and had children, I had started writing children's picture book stories and continued to do so as the kids grew up. I even wrote a picture book story when my first granddaughter was born, but I never seriously took my love for writing to the next level. To be honest, I occasionally dipped my feet in the water, so to speak, and I sent manuscripts off to publishing houses over the years. I've even received plenty of rejection letters. However, I didn't think about it too much.

Of course, now that has changed. What's different is that I've come to realize that I'm passionate about writing, and it is through this recognition of my passion that I've been led directly to the discovery of my purpose. And all of this happened while in the midst of chaos. When the mental illness of our daughter came crashing down on us, like it did, the way that I healed, and continue to heal, is through writing. Interesting, isn't it? And instead of sending manuscripts off to publishing houses, I've taken publishing into my own hands. Years ago, I never would have dreamt that I'd do this, but I have. I have discovered my passion and purpose.

Regarding the discovery of my passion and purpose in life, after Kim's last suicide attempt, I found myself coping by writing late at night while everyone else slept. The result of my writing, during that difficult time, is a memoir that I wrote. Why am I sharing this with you now? I tend to believe, (Remember, these are simply 1 mom's thoughts!) it's during times of crisis that we can discover what it is that we are passionate about doing.

I think that it's important that I share with you that I'm a realist, and as such, I realize that this just doesn't happen for everyone during a challenging time in their life. I've experienced many challenging times in my life, and I didn't experience an "aha" moment. However, for me, Kim's last suicide attempt spun me in a new direction. What I experienced, as a mother, redefined me in a significant manner. I don't want to dismiss this as I share my story with you just in case it can be of help to you.

I imagine that you are wondering what my rationale is in regard to my thinking that growth can occur during difficult times. My reasoning is that when faced with great challenge, we oftentimes react by doing what it is that we are so good at doing. I have proof. I reacted to Kim's last, near fatal, suicide attempt by writing which is what I'm passionate about doing. Bill reacted by updating Kim's room with a splash of lavender color, new hardwood flooring and new decorations. At that time, he even invited Paul and Katlin to partake in the room renovation. He wanted Kim to feel loved and welcomed when she came home from the hospital, and he wanted her have a space that would promote healing for her. His approach was threefold. In addition to welcoming Kim home and sharing with her how much he loves her, and providing her with a healing space, he also wanted to help Paul and Katlin begin the long journey of healing as well. He provided the means for Paul and Katlin to heal through brushstrokes. With each brushstroke of lavender paint that was applied to Kim's walls by Bill, Paul and Katlin, healing was in full swing.

Did I share with you yet, Bill's passion is to create special spaces for people? Furthermore, when we brought Kim home from the hospital, she started to sing once again which is her passion. Paul and Katlin returned to their lives to pursue their passions. Life didn't end after all. It had actually just begun, once again, like a new chapter in a book.

I invite you to think about what it is that you are passionate about doing. Is it healthy? Do it! You are worth it, and you know what's so great and helpful about this? You will gain renewed energy and strength to continue to fight the good fight with your loved one, and what's especially important is that you will be able to provide helpful and meaningful support to your adult child, when, and if, needed.

12

There Is Hope

In closing, I'd like to share with you that there is so much hope for our adult children who live with the challenges of mental illness. It can be easy to view mental illness negatively, especially when stigma clouds our judgement. However, it doesn't have to be like that. Yes, mental illness, just like any illness, can be unpleasant. When a person doesn't feel well, whether they don't feel well physically or mentally, they just don't feel well. That is when we know that it might be time to visit with a doctor or therapist. And getting help is okay. That's what we want to express to our children. We want to express that it's okay to reach out for help, and many times, as parents of an adult child, that's all we can do. As much as we want to, we can't make our adult children seek help, but what we can do is encourage our child to seek help, and we can provide all the love and support that we possibly can.

Important to note, if your adult child is a harm to self or others, I highly encourage you to call 911 or take your child to an emergency room. And remember, if you call 911, ask for a Crisis Intervention Trained (CIT) officer who is trained in such emergencies. More details and resources, regarding seeking help for your adult child, are provided at the end of the book in the sections titled "6 Tips I Wish Someone Would Have Shared With Me" and "Resources."

In regard to providing your adult child with the help and support that he or she may need now or in the future, the National Alliance on Mental Illness (NAMI) provides a helpful guide titled Family Members and Caregivers. I highly encourage you to read this guide. The guide includes the following sections and several other sections as well: Learning to Help Your Child and Your Family, Supporting Recovery, Maintaining a Healthy Relationship, and Calling 911 and Talking with Police.

Also, I can't express enough how important it is that we learn how to communicate with our loved ones. Don't get me wrong here. I'm not saying that anyone who lives with mental illness communicates differently. I'm just saying that now, more than ever, is the time to learn how to communicate in the most effective manner so that you can help your adult child. Communication can be key to getting our children the help that they need so let's make sure we communicate the best we can. The Depression and Bipolar Support Alliance (DBSA) provides several guides that help us do just that. I've included them below, and I highly encourage you to check them out. They are a quick read, and if you take the time to read the guides, and apply what you learn, you will help set yourself up for success when you communicate with your loved one. I think you will agree that the 30 minutes or so that it takes to read the DBSA guides will be minutes well spent. The 30 minutes or so can turn into the gift of a lifetime for someone else. I encourage you to talk with a doctor or therapist about this as well. He or she may have additional ideas on how best to communicate with your child. The guides I recommend include:

- Helping Others Throughout Their Lives: What Can I do When my Child is Ill?

- How to Help in a Crisis

- Psychiatric Hospitalization: A Guide for Families

- What Helps and What Hurts

At this point in the book, I don't think it would be right if I didn't share with you how Kim is doing, and I imagine that you are wondering this as well. I'm happy to share with you that she is doing remarkably well, and so are we. She is busy tending to her beautiful daughter now, and in addition, she is still singing and working towards fulfilling her dream of becoming a singer. You can actually see and hear her perform on her YouTube channel titled, Kim King. She'd love it if you stopped by to see her, and any support you have to offer her would be priceless to her and me.

Lastly, I am closing this chapter with a Stacy's Flutterings blog snapshot that focuses on erasing the stigma of mental illness—and it's also about finding hope. The documentary, which Kim and I were a part of, and that is talked about in this particular blog post, is no longer available. Regardless, I want to share this blog post with you because I think that it gets to the heart of hope.

I hope you've found this book to be helpful, and I hope you can use it as a resource as you journey you're your loved one. You can always find me over at stacysflutterings.com.

Until we meet again! My hat is off to you for the remarkable job you are doing as a parent. The fact that you are reading these very words is evidence that you care and love your adult child very much. How could reading possibly be evidence? Reading is proof that you are reaching out for information. If you didn't care, I don't think you'd be here. Keep growing! I'm sending positive thoughts and energy your way!

SPOTLIGHT ON ERASING THE STIGMA

January 19, 2012

Sometimes, just like the transformation of a delicate, beautiful butterfly with iridescent colored wings, the very things that matter most to many of us like our family, our friends, change, acceptance and support take a while to grow. We plant the seed…we wait for it to take hold. We nurture…we watch. We tend to…we love. We prompt…and we patiently wait and hold onto hope. And then, just like the butterfly, the very thing we were growing slowly and miraculously unfolds.

Erasing the stigma is one such thing that is near and dear to my heart as it is to many others. And it is slowly unfolding as people talk more about it, and it's being erased one person at a time. One step my family and I have taken to erase the stigma is that we talk openly about mental illness, the challenges we face and how we cope as a family of a loved one with bipolar disorder. And our loved one also desires to talk about living with bipolar disorder, and with time and support, I am sure she will become an advocate helping others who walk the same walk.

It's not easy being an open book. There is this overwhelming sense of vulnerability that I sometimes feel that accompanies being open about mental illness and its effects. I also have a gnawing sense of guilt. I call it mommy guilt. My mommy guilt thermometer rises as I find myself asking the question, "How can I put my family on the front-line of something so vast?" And then I remember why. It is for the very ones I love and the immeasurable number of others who are affected by stigma. After all, we can't just put stigma aside and expect for it to fade away. Like the documentary points out, 1 in 6 Americans is experiencing a mental illness this year. Furthermore, stigma about mental illness prevents half of those with mental illness from seeking treatment.

To that end, Kim and I accepted an invitation to participate in the MICDS documentary titled: Living with Mental Illness: People are More than Patients. After weeks of preparation, students' Anna, Chris and Darryl's Mental Illness Documentary is complete. It includes a segment from a Charlie Sheen interview and interviews with Tom, Fran and Kevin Smith of the Karla Smith Foundation, advocate Ellen Rosenbaum, Arlen Chaleff, Vice President of NAMI St. Louis, myself and Kim singing since she wasn't present. She sings "Mercy on Me" by Christina Aguilera, and at one point viewers will hear Kim singing "Save Me from Myself" also by Christina Aguilera. These particular recordings are from 2007.

They did an excellent job of capturing the humanness of mental illness through the lens of families affected by mental illness and suicide and those who have and still struggle with emotional disorders. They also did a beautiful job of showcasing the strengths and potential of someone with a mental illness. Ellen Fein Rosenbaum is a past honoree of the Ten Outstanding Young Americans annual award along with honorees such as John F. Kennedy, Elvis and Bill Clinton. Arlen Chaleff, Vice President of NAMI St. Louis, was one of four chosen for the St. Louis 2009 Women of Achievement Award. And then...there is Kim. She was our song bird, and as I mentioned in the interview, she seems to have lost her voice for now, but we have hope that she will regain balance and pursue her interests once again. Just like the butterfly...it may take some time. We tend to...we love. We prompt...and we patiently wait and hold onto hope...

Sadly, Kim was not present for the interview as she had hoped she would be She didn't make it home the night before. When morning made its grand arrival, and I wandered into Kim's room, I discovered her bed was empty. In that moment, I thought about calling Anna and canceling my part of the interview. Then I thought...wait a minute...this is "our normal" so why not do the interview after all. When Anna and her classmates arrived for the interview, excited to meet Kim, I gave them the news. I felt like we had let them down. However, it became a teachable moment. I shared with them that she sometimes self-medicates and that that was what probably happened. I also shared that we actually live each day not knowing what's to come. With that, we did the interview. I wish Kim would have been there. She did show up later that day, and thankfully she was safe.

We tend to…we love. We prompt…and we patiently wait and hold onto hope…

6 Tips I Wish Someone Would Have Shared With Me

1). Lock up medications, firearms and any other items that could be used in a harmful manner. As you know, I learned this the hard way. And even though my loved one overdosed on a volatile mix of psychotropic medications, not one person told me to take preventative measures after the fact. In reality, I didn't need to be told this, and I indeed bought and use a locking box for medications. But it seemed I was left to my own devices when it came to suicide prevention. But it didn't have to be that way. The National Suicide Prevention Lifeline offers a guide online that you might find useful titled Use The Do's and Don'ts. I encourage you to check it out.

2). I can't express enough how much personal therapy has helped me. If you are the parent of an adult child who lives with mental illness, I encourage you to give personal therapy a try. At the very least, you may learn additional coping methods that you can add to your parenting toolbox, and you may learn about local resources that may be of help to you and your child. If you find that you are searching for a therapist, I recommend the American Association for Marriage and Family Therapy (AAMFT) Therapist Locator. If you live outside of the United States, I encourage you to reach out to your primary care provider for a referral.

3). If your child is 18 years old, or older, and you have concerns that you'd like to share with your adult child's treatment team, and your child hasn't signed a Release of Information document allowing his or her treatment to talk with you, you can still communicate your concerns to his or her treatment team. However, you may have to get creative. First, if this is of concern, I encourage you to contact the office staff in the doctor and/or therapist's office and inquire about what steps you can take, as a loved one, to report concerns. The office staff should be able to share with you the doctor and/or therapist's rules for reporting concerns.

If you find that you've hit a roadblock and can't report your concerns, due to the rules of confidentiality, you can try writing a letter to the doctor and/or therapist. You then can deliver the letter to the front office clerk. You may find that you can use email as well, but it will depend on the doctor and/or therapist's rules. I've written letters on occasion, to express my concerns about Kim's mental health, and believe me, it helped. The catch here is that, even though the doctor and/or therapist can't talk to you, due to the rules of confidentiality, he or she can certainly read a letter or note. It's always a good idea, as well, to address this concern with your child. You never know. He or she may be willing to sign the Release of Information document allowing his or her doctor and/or therapist to talk to you. It's worth a try. Kim and I have had this conversation, and in the past, she made sure and put my name down.

4). If you find that your adult child is exhibiting behavior that you are concerned about, especially if your adult child happens to live at home with you, I encourage you to write your concerns down. You can actually use something as simple as a calendar to jot down concerns or you can create a journal. I like to use a timeline and add side notes. Regardless of what you decide to do, your notes might come in handy if you decide to talk to a doctor or therapist about your child's behavior. You might be able to provide valuable insight that your child's treatment team may not be aware of and that your adult child may not be aware of either because of his or her illness.

5). If your adult child becomes a harm to self or others, and you find yourself calling 911, try and remember that there are officers who are trained on how to respond to these types of situations. Don't be afraid to ask for a Crisis Intervention Trained (CIT) officer. Of course, I don't know what the rules are across the globe, but if you happen to live outside of the United States, I encourage you to do some research about this very important topic. Remember, if you make an emergency call, the dispatcher should be able to match your needs with an appropriately trained officer.

6). As the parent of an adult child who lives with mental illness, you are one of your child's greatest advocates, and as such, you can work to erase the stigma of mental illness which in turn will benefit your child and benefit all people who live with mental illness. You have so much to offer as an advocate because you've been there, you know what works, and you know what doesn't. Why not share your knowledge to help eradicate the stigma that is so entrenched in our society? You can make a difference. And just maybe this is part of your purpose. If not, that's okay, but it's something to consider.

Helpful Resources

American Association for Marriage and Family Therapy (AAMFT)

Active Minds

Bring Change 2 Mind

Care for Your Mind

Crisis Text Line

Depression and Bipolar Support Alliance (DBSA)

National Alliance on Mental Illness (NAMI)

National Suicide Prevention Lifeline

The Balanced Mind Parent Network

Note from the Author

If you or someone you know is in crisis, the National Suicide Prevention Lifeline is available 24/7. The phone number is 1-800-273-8255, and they are available to chat on line as well.

Thank you for reading. If you've found this book to be helpful, please consider leaving an honest review on Amazon.com.

And if you find that stigma is stopping you from leaving a review, I hope you'll take the leap and leave a review anyway in an effort to get the word out to other parents who might benefit from this guide. Let's erase the stigma, get the conversation going and get resources into the hands of those who need them.

Also, to reach me and keep up-to-date on book releases and other news, you can always find me here:

Stacysflutterings.com
Amazon
BookBub
Goodreads

Stacy - Simply 1 Mom

References

- ARCH National Respite Network and Resource Center. Accessed on November 4, 2015 at http://archrespite.org/

- Association for Psychological Science. (2011, December 29). "The Silver Lining To Adversity." Medical News Today. Retrieved from http://www.medicalnewstoday.com/releases/2394 17.php

- Francis Bacon. (n.d.). BrainyQuote.com. Retrieved November 20, 2015, from BrainyQuote.com Web site: http://www.brainyquote.com/quotes/quotes/f/fran cisbac100764

- Frankl, V. (n.d.). BrainyQuote.com. Retrieved November 20, 2015, from BrainyQuote.com Web site: http://www.brainyquote.com/quotes/quotes/v/vikt orefr121087.html

- Harris, S. (n.d.). BrainyQuote.com. Retrieved November 20, 2015, from BrainyQuote.com Web site:

- http://www.brainyquote.com/quotes/quotes/s/sydn eyjha152325.html

- Khaleghi, K. (July 11, 2012). Are you empowering or enabling. Retrieved from http://www.psychologytoday.com/blog/the-anatomy-addiction/201207/are-you-empowering-or-enabling

- King, S. (2015). [Stacy's Flutterings Blog]. Retrieved from http://stacysflutterings.com/

- Merriam-Webster Dictionary Online. Accessed on November 4, 2015 at http://www.merriam-webster.com/dictionary/respite

- World Health Organization. (2015). Mental disorders [Fact Sheet]. Retrieved from http://www.who.int/mediacentre/factsheets/fs396/en/

Made in the USA
Middletown, DE
30 November 2021

53813316R00050